SUMMARY OF THE LATTER GLORY OF GOD REVEALED

How to Walk Under the Blessing of the Glory Cloud

GUILLERMO MALDONADO

D DESTINY IMAGE

Destiny Image P.O. Box 310, Shippensburg, PA 17257-0310

This book and all other Destiny Image's books are available at Christian bookstores and distributors worldwide.

For Worldwide Distribution.

Reach us on the Internet: www.destinyimage.com.

ISBN 13 TP: 9798881500870

ISBN 13 eBook: 9798881500887

CONTENTS

INTRODUCTION

In "The Latter Glory of God Revealed," this compelling book offers an exploration into the profound narrative of God's eternal glory as it moves from biblical times to the present day. Through a tapestry of scriptural references, personal testimonies, and theological insights, the author illustrates how the glory once housed in the Ark of the Covenant now dynamically resides within the global body of believers. Each section of the book is designed to deepen understanding and inspire believers to become active carriers of God's glory, showcasing its transformative impact on individual lives and communities. This summary encapsulates the key principles, stories, and calls to action that beckon every reader to partake in the ongoing story of God's magnificent glory.

CHAPTER 1
ICHABOD, THE LOST GLORY

Bible Verse

"Remember therefore from where you have fallen; repent and do the first works, or else I will come to you quickly and remove your lampstand from its place—unless you repent." (Revelation 2:5)

Introduction

In "Ichabod, the Lost Glory," the author navigates the critical nature of the current spiritual epoch, termed as the "end time," urging believers to awaken from spiritual lethargy, return to true worship, and embrace the latter glory of God. This call to action is vital to prepare for Jesus' second coming and the full manifestation of God's glory.

Word of Wisdom

"Sadly, I have seen entire denominations that are dead and spiritually dry, displaying residues of their past glory,

which is no longer there." Guillermo Maldonado

Main Theme

The chapter warns against the dangers of falling away from God's presence, illustrated by the biblical account of Israel losing the Ark of the Covenant. It underscores the urgent need for revival within the church through a true restoration of God's glory.

Key Points

- Living in the "end times" requires a heightened awareness and readiness among Christians.
- The loss of the Ark in Israel serves as a historical and spiritual parallel to today's church losing God's glory.
- Restoration involves reconnecting with the Holy Spirit and rejecting superficial religiosity.
- True encounters with God's glory transform believers and empower them to overcome spiritual darkness.
- Testimonies of miracles and supernatural occurrences underscore the tangible presence of God's glory.
- The church's current state often reflects an "Ichabod" scenario, indicating the departure of God's glory due to sin and disobedience.

Key Themes

- **The Concept of Latter Glory:** The chapter explores the promised latter glory of God, which signifies a profound and final manifestation of divine presence and power. Believers are called to transition from the first glory to this latter glory through deep spiritual renewal and obedience.
- **Historical Context of Ichabod:** The term "Ichabod" reflects a critical moment in Israel's history where they lost the tangible presence of God due to disobedience and moral decay, paralleling the modern church's spiritual challenges.
- **Impact of Supernatural Encounters:** Testimonies shared from various ministries reveal how supernatural encounters with God's glory have led to healing, conversions, and spiritual revival, even under oppressive conditions.
- **Warnings from Spiritual Leadership:** The insights from Prophet Glenda Jackson about the state of many churches today serve as a dire warning that without repentance, many will continue to operate without the true presence of God.
- **Restoration Through Repentance:** The chapter emphasizes that the path to recovering God's glory is through genuine repentance, heartfelt worship, and a continual seeking of God's face.

Conclusion

"Ichabod, the Lost Glory" serves as a sober reminder and a call to action for the church to awaken from complacency and restore the glory of God in their midst. By returning to foundational spiritual practices and seeking a genuine relationship with God, believers can reclaim the divine presence that once defined and empowered the church.

CHAPTER 2

LEADING CAUSES FOR ICHABOD IN THE CHURCH

Bible Verse

"For all have sinned and fall short of the glory of God." (Romans 3:23)

Introduction

This chapter delves into the reasons behind the departure of God's glory from the Church, likened to the biblical concept of Ichabod. Through a series of poignant testimonies and biblical narratives, the author explicates the spiritual decline that results from sin, iniquity, moral corruption, and compromise, urging a return to foundational Christian values and practices.

Word of Wisdom

"The purpose of sin is to remove man from the glory of God." Guillermo Maldonado

. . .

Main Theme

The central theme explores the primary reasons for the loss of divine glory in the Church, highlighting sin and iniquity, moral decay in leadership, compromise of biblical truths, and the erosion of the fear of God.

Key Points

- Miraculous testimonies contrast sharply with the Church's current spiritual state, illustrating the power of God's presence.
- Sin and iniquity are identified as foundational issues causing spiritual separation from God.
- Moral corruption in church leadership directly contributes to a loss of divine glory.
- Compromising biblical truths for personal gain leads to a departure of God's glory.
- The diminishing fear of God among believers and leaders alike exacerbates the decline.
- A call for repentance and restoration of biblical principles is urgently presented.

Key Themes

- **Sin and Iniquity's Role in Spiritual Decline:** The author discusses how original sin and ongoing disobedience remove individuals and congregations from God's presence. This separation results not just from overt actions but from deep-seated moral corruption within one's heart.

- **Corruption in Church Leadership:** Drawing parallels with the biblical priesthood, the chapter argues that current leadership often mirrors these failings, leading to widespread spiritual decay and loss of credibility in the Church.
- **The Dangers of Compromise:** By yielding to societal pressures and personal desires, church leaders compromise God's truth, which slowly erodes the church's spiritual foundation and diminishes its glory.
- **Loss of the Fear of God:** The chapter stresses that a lack of reverence for God's holiness and authority is a critical issue facing today's Church, leading to casual and irreverent attitudes towards sacred doctrines.
- **Call for Restoration:** Urging a return to strict adherence to biblical doctrines and a renewed reverence for God, the author believes that these steps are essential for the revival of God's glory within the Church.

Conclusion

The departure of God's glory from the Church, symbolized by Ichabod, serves as a dire warning and a call to action for all believers. This chapter implores the Church to confront and rectify the sins, iniquities, and compromises that have led to its current state. By embracing repentance and re-instating the fear of God, the Church can hope to recover the lost glory and experience a renewed divine presence.

CHAPTER 3

BRING BACK THE CHABOD OF GOD

Bible Verse

"But your iniquities have separated you from your God; and your sins have hidden His face from you, so that He will not hear." (Isaiah 59:2)

Introduction

This chapter emphasizes the urgent need for the Church to restore God's glory, lost through sin and disobedience. Drawing parallels with the early Christian Church, which thrived despite persecution because of its purity and connection to God, the author discusses how the modern Church can reclaim this divine glory.

Word of Wisdom

"Sin cannot enter the realm of the glory of God; therefore, if it dwells in us,

God's glory will not dwell in our spirit."
Guillermo Maldonado

Main Theme

The primary focus is on understanding the profound effects of losing God's glory due to sin and outlining steps to reclaim this lost divine presence, thereby revitalizing the Church's spiritual power and impact.

Key Points

- The early Church thrived due to its direct and profound connection to God's glory.
- Sin and its consequences directly cause the loss of divine presence.
- Reclaiming God's glory requires sincere repentance and a return to biblical principles.
- The presence of God's glory is both visible and tangible, affecting all aspects of life.
- Unrepentant sin results in spiritual nakedness and vulnerability to satanic attacks.
- True repentance leads to a restored relationship with God and the return of His protective glory.

Key Themes

- **Consequences of Losing God's Glory:** The aftermath of living in sin is profound, leading to unanswered prayers and spiritual exposure. The author emphasizes that just as God selectively revealed His glory historically, He continues to do so, withdrawing it in the presence of sin.

- **The Protective Nature of God's Glory:** The glory of God acts as a hedge of protection. Without it, believers are exposed to spiritual and physical dangers. This lack of protection was starkly illustrated in the life of Job when God removed His protective hedge.
- **Religiosity versus True Spirituality:** A life devoid of God's glory is marked by religiosity, which lacks the power and presence of God. The author distinguishes between mere religious formality and the transformative power of true spiritual engagement.
- **The Tangibility of God's Presence:** The author stresses that God's presence is not an abstract concept but a tangible reality that should manifest in healing, deliverance, and spiritual renewal. When sin blocks this presence, the spiritual life of a believer becomes barren.
- **The Imperative of Repentance:** Detailed steps towards repentance are discussed, stressing that genuine change in behavior and attitude is necessary to restore God's glory. The author calls for a revival of true repentance within the Church to overcome spiritual decay.

Conclusion

"Bring Back the Chabod of God" serves as a clarion call to the Church to confront and eradicate sin through deep, sincere repentance. By doing so, the Church can experience a revival of God's tangible presence and power, leading to spiritual renewal and transformation in the lives of believers.

CHAPTER 4

THE RESTORATION OF THE GLORY

Bible Verse

"Repent therefore and be converted, that your sins may be blotted out, so that times of refreshing may come from the presence of the Lord." (Acts 3:19)

Introduction

This chapter delves into the biblical concept of restoration to the original glory of God that humanity once enjoyed. The author underscores the need for repentance and spiritual renewal to return to this state, drawing parallels between the early church's experiences and the modern call for revival.

Word of Wisdom

"Jesus came to restore the glory of the Father and will soon return for a glorious church." Guillermo Maldonado

Main Theme

The theme focuses on understanding and facilitating the restoration of God's glory in the lives of believers and the Church, emphasizing that this restoration is central to God's plan for the end times.

Key Points

- Humanity originally lived in a state of divine glory, which was lost due to sin.
- Restoration to this glory is essential and achievable through repentance.
- The end times will feature a significant restoration of God's glory among believers.
- Miraculous signs and wonders, such as those witnessed on mission trips, exemplify God's glory.
- Jesus Christ is central to the restoration process as the manifest glory of God.
- The modern Church must actively pursue a restoration of this glory through genuine spiritual commitment.

Key Themes

- **Definition and Importance of Restoration:** Restoration involves returning something to its original or proper condition. For humanity, this means returning to the original state of living in God's glory, which requires repentance and a turning away from sin.

- **Biblical Basis for Restoration:** The author provides scriptural references to illustrate that God's plan has always included restoring His people to glory, especially highlighted through the prophecies and the ministry of Jesus Christ.
- **Role of Jesus in Restoration:** Jesus Christ is depicted not just as a savior but as the ultimate restoration of God's glory to humanity. His life, death, and resurrection are central to God's plan for bringing all things back to their intended glory.
- **Practical Implications of Restoration:** The presence of God's glory has tangible effects on individuals and communities, such as protection, spiritual power, and guidance, which were evident during the author's mission trips where many experienced miraculous changes.
- **Urgency of the Restoration Process:** The current global crises and moral decay underscore the urgent need for the Church to seek and facilitate the restoration of God's glory through deep, corporate repentance and a recommitment to living out biblical truths.

Conclusion

"The Restoration of the Glory" calls for a decisive return to the principles and power that characterized the early Church. By embracing repentance and recommitting to Christ's lordship, believers can experience a renewed manifestation of God's glory, preparing the Church for its role in the end times and the return of Christ.

CHAPTER 5

THE EARTH WILL BE
FILLED WITH HIS GLORY

Bible Verse

"For the earth will be filled with the knowledge of the glory of the Lord, as the waters cover the sea."
(Habakkuk 2:14)

Introduction

This chapter explores the promise of God's glory covering the earth, evidenced by miraculous events and transformations witnessed by the author, particularly during a mission in Chiapas, Mexico. It stresses the role of the Church in manifesting this glory through faith and obedience.

Word of Wisdom

"The Glory is the closing act; it is God's curtains down on earth in this end time." Guillermo Maldonado

Main Theme

The chapter underscores the biblical promise that God's glory will envelop the entire earth, transforming lives through supernatural interventions and the Church's faithful ministry.

Key Points

- The glory of God transforms individuals and communities, bringing about miraculous healings and spiritual renewals.
- The presence of God's glory is a catalyst for dramatic change, capable of reversing physical and spiritual afflictions.
- God's glory will increasingly manifest in the end times, showcasing divine preservation and health among His people.
- Darkness in the world will be counteracted by the rising glory of God through His people.
- The Church is called to live out and spread this glory as a testimony to God's power and sovereignty.

Key Themes

- **Transformation Through Glory:** The glory of God not only signifies His presence but actively transforms lives—alcoholics find sobriety, the sick are healed, and broken relationships are mended. This transformative power was vividly demonstrated in Chiapas, where individual lives were miraculously changed.

- **Supernatural Manifestations as a Testament:** The author recounts instances where God's glory was visibly and tangibly manifested, such as the creation of new organs and the healing of long-standing physical ailments. These events serve as a testament to the divine power and presence of God.

- **Scriptural Foundation for God's Glory:** Biblical references throughout the chapter highlight the scriptural basis for believing in and expecting the manifestation of God's glory, with citations from Haggai, Corinthians, and Isaiah illustrating how historical prophecies and teachings support this expectation.

- **Practical Implications for Believers:** Believers are encouraged to expect and facilitate the manifestation of God's glory in their own lives by living in obedience and purity. The chapter calls for a lifestyle that reflects God's holiness and power, preparing believers for their role in the end times.

- **Anticipation of Global Impact:** The chapter posits that as darkness increases globally, the glory of God will likewise intensify, leading to global changes that will prepare the world for Christ's return. This glory is not just for personal transformation but is pivotal in God's plan for the world.

Conclusion

The chapter concludes with a call to action for believers to rise up and embrace their calling to manifest God's glory. By living lives that radiate His power and love, believers will play a critical role in fulfilling the prophecy that God's glory will fill the earth, transforming it as completely as waters cover the sea.

CHAPTER 6

THE LATTER GLORY REVEALED

Bible Verse

"The earth will be filled with the knowledge of the glory of the Lord as the waters cover the sea." (Habakkuk 2:14)

Introduction

This chapter delves into the concept of divine glory, emphasizing that understanding and experiencing God's glory requires a spiritual revelation, not mere intellectual reasoning. It describes transformative experiences from global ministry events where the latter glory of God was manifested.

Word of Wisdom

"The essence of the nature of God is His glory and is demonstrated by His supernatural works." Guillermo Maldonado

Main Theme

The theme explores the profound nature of God's glory, illustrating how it transcends human understanding and manifests through miraculous works, changing lives and restoring people physically and spiritually.

Key Points

- Revelation of God's glory is essential for truly experiencing and walking in it.
- God's nature is described as supernatural, demanding worship and characterized by infinite holiness, justice, and goodness.
- The glory of God is distinctly different from worldly glory, which is transient and ego-driven.
- True divine glory manifests in tangible, miraculous outcomes during worship and ministry.
- Understanding the nature of God and His glory requires spiritual revelation, not intellectual deduction.
- The latter glory of God promises even greater manifestations of God's power and presence than ever before.

Key Themes

- **Nature and Revelation of God:** God's essence is supernatural and beyond human comparison, revealed not through human reasoning but through spiritual enlightenment. This chapter outlines how a deeper understanding of God's nature can lead to more profound experiences of His glory.

- **Manifestations of God's Glory:** True divine glory manifests in miraculous healings and transformations, significantly different from the temporary and superficial glory sought in the secular world. These manifestations are physical evidences of spiritual truths.
- **Distinguishing Divine Glory:** It's critical to differentiate between God's eternal, supernatural glory and the fleeting glories of human achievement or admiration. The chapter stresses that focusing on God's glory leads to lasting spiritual fulfillment and transformation.
- **Impact of God's Glory in Ministry:** The chapter recounts several powerful testimonies from ministry events where individuals experienced dramatic healings and conversions, underscoring the tangible impact of God's glory when it is genuinely manifested.
- **Preparing for Greater Glory:** In anticipation of the end times, believers are called to deepen their understanding and experience of God's glory, which is integral to manifesting His power on earth and fulfilling divine purposes.

Conclusion

The chapter concludes with a call to action for believers to seek a deeper revelation of God's glory, preparing them to live out and demonstrate this glory in a world filled with darkness and challenges. It emphasizes that the church must rise to the occasion, embodying the fullness of God's glory as it prepares for the return of Christ.

CHAPTER 7

JESUS IS THE GLORY OF THE LORD

Bible Verse

"Who is this King of glory? The Lord strong and mighty, the Lord mighty in battle." (Psalm 24:8)

Introduction

This chapter explores the concept of kingship in a biblical context, emphasizing that Jesus Christ embodies the ultimate King, holding dominion over all creation, visible and invisible. His reign as the King of kings reveals the full glory of God.

Word of Wisdom

"Jesus is the glory of God revealed to us in this end time." Guillermo Maldonado

Main Theme

The theme centers on understanding Jesus' sovereignty as the King of glory, whose authority surpasses all earthly and spiritual rulers. It delves into how Jesus' kingship represents the full manifestation of God's glory.

Key Points

• Jesus exercises sovereign authority over all creation.

• His kingship is an eternal and unchallengeable rule.

• Jesus is recognized as the King of kings both now and in the age to come.

• Every ruler and authority must submit to Jesus' supremacy.

• Jesus' rule is characterized by His absolute power and glory.

• Understanding Jesus' kingship is essential to comprehending the nature of God's kingdom.

Key Themes

• **Concept of Kingship:** In the Bible, kingship is linked with authority and territory. Jesus, as the King, has authority over heaven, earth, and under the earth, signifying His ultimate rule over all realms.

• **Jesus' Sovereign Rule:** Jesus' authority is not just over the physical realm but also extends to the spiritual, where He has dominion over all principalities and powers. This supreme authority was established through His resurrection and is eternal.

- **The Nature of God's Glory:** God's glory is fundamentally different from human glory, which is fleeting and often ego-driven. Jesus, as the embodiment of God's glory, represents an eternal, transformative power that affects all creation.
- **Manifestations of Glory Through Jesus:** The miracles and acts of Jesus throughout the Gospels demonstrate that the glory of God is not an abstract concept but a tangible reality manifested through Christ's actions on earth.
- **Relational Aspect of Jesus' Kingship:** Understanding Jesus as the King of glory involves recognizing His ongoing relationship with humanity. His rule is not distant but is marked by His interaction with His creation, particularly in manifesting salvation and miracles.

Conclusion

Jesus Christ is the ultimate revelation of God's glory. By recognizing Jesus as the sovereign King, believers can understand the true nature of authority and glory. This acknowledgment transforms how we view our own lives and challenges, encouraging us to live under His reign and to expect His sovereign acts in our lives.

CHAPTER 8

CHARACTERISTICS OF THE GLORY

Bible Verse

"And the glory of the Lord will be revealed, and all people will see it together. For the mouth of the Lord has spoken." (Isaiah 40:5 NIV)

Introduction

This chapter delves into the multifaceted characteristics of God's glory as manifested through Jesus Christ. It explores how the glory of God, embodying all of God's attributes, sovereignty, and power, is revealed in creation and rest, and how it influences our interaction with the divine.

Word of Wisdom

"Glory is all that God is and manifests at a precise moment in time."
Guillermo Maldonado

Main Theme

The theme centers on the diverse characteristics of God's glory, revealing how it functions within the realms of creation, rest, and personal experience, impacting both the physical and spiritual aspects of life.

Key Points

• Glory encompasses all aspects of God's being and is manifested in His creative works.

• God's glory operates within a realm of rest, promoting a state of spiritual peace and trust.

• The glory of God is intensely personal yet universally pervasive, impacting individuals and the global church.

• Understanding and experiencing God's glory requires a revelation of its nature.

• Resting in God's glory involves a deep, abiding trust in His sovereignty and timing.

Key Themes

- **Glory as Creation:** The glory of God is fundamentally creative, responsible for miraculous occurrences like spontaneous healings and the creation of organs. This creative power is an intrinsic aspect of God's glory that manifests when faith and conditions allow.
- **Restorative Nature of Glory:** True rest in the context of God's glory isn't mere

inactivity but a profound state of spiritual and emotional peace where believers trust wholly in God's sovereignty, reflecting deep biblical concepts of Sabbath and divine rest.

- **Personal Experience with Glory:** Each believer's interaction with God's glory is personal, requiring individual revelation and transformation. This personal aspect underscores the intimacy and transformative potential of encountering God's glory.
- **Global and Corporate Impact:** While the glory of God transforms individuals, it also has a corporate dimension, filling congregations and manifesting globally, showcasing the pervasive and inclusive nature of divine glory.
- **Visibility and Tangibility:** The glory of God is not abstract but can be seen and felt, impacting the senses and demonstrating that the supernatural can indeed penetrate the natural realm.

Conclusion

The glory of God, as described through the person of Jesus Christ, encompasses a broad spectrum of divine characteristics, from creation to rest, and from personal revelation to global impact. Believers are called to recognize and rest in this glory, allowing it to transform them and the world around them, ushering in a profound understanding and experience of God's omnipresence and sovereignty.

CHAPTER 9

TRANSITIONING FROM THE FIRST TO THE LATTER GLORY

Bible Verse

"Eye has not seen, nor ear heard, nor have entered into the heart of man the things which God has prepared for those who love Him." (1 Corinthians 2:9)

Introduction

This chapter explores the transition from the first to the latter glory within the Church, emphasizing the necessity of recognizing and embracing this spiritual shift to experience deeper manifestations of God's presence and power.

Word of Wisdom

"Declare it! The latter glory has already started in your life." Guillermo Maldonado

Main Theme

The main theme focuses on the progression from a previous season of divine interaction, termed the "first glory," to a new and more powerful "latter glory," which involves a broader, deeper encounter with God's supernatural presence and work.

Key Points

• God directly communicates the need for a transition in glory within the Church.

• The first glory includes foundational works and past revivals.

• A transition to the latter glory is marked by new miracles and deeper encounters with God.

• Recognizing and declaring this transition is crucial for its realization.

• Challenges and resistance often accompany the shift from the first to the latter glory.

Key Themes

• **Understanding of Transition:**
Transitioning from the first to the latter glory is a divine mandate that requires recognition and declaration. This shift is necessary for the Church to experience greater depths of God's power and presence.
• **Manifestations of the Latter Glory:**
The latter glory is characterized by

unprecedented miracles and spiritual breakthroughs, which exceed those witnessed in the first glory, emphasizing the continual growth and renewal in God's plans for His people.

- **Resistance to Change:** The transition between glories often meets with resistance, both spiritually and culturally, within the Church. Understanding and overcoming this resistance is essential for moving forward into the new things God has prepared.
- **Significance of Declarations:** Declarations play a crucial role in the spiritual realm, setting into motion the changes decreed by God. This prophetic act impacts both heavenly and earthly realms, aligning them with God's will.
- **Necessity of Discernment:** Discerning the timing and nature of the transition from the first to the latter glory is critical. Without this discernment, individuals and congregations risk missing the move of God and remaining in a past season.

Conclusion

The transition from the first to the latter glory is a pivotal process that requires active engagement, spiritual sensitivity, and a readiness to embrace God's new movements. This chapter calls believers to recognize their role in this divine shift, encouraging them to step into the greater works and deeper manifestations of God's glory.

࿇

CHAPTER 10

HOW TO TRANSITION TO THE LATTER GLORY

Bible Verse

"But we all, with unveiled face, beholding as in a mirror the glory of the Lord, are being transformed into the same image from glory to glory, just as by the Spirit of the Lord." (2 Corinthians 3:18)

Introduction

This chapter delves into the essential changes and preparations required to transition into the latter glory, emphasizing personal transformation and the relinquishing of old paradigms to embrace God's supernatural realm.

Word of Wisdom

"Change is the key to making the transition to the latter glory." Guillermo Maldonado

Main Theme

Transitioning to the latter glory requires a fundamental change in mindset and behavior, aligning oneself with God's desires and the workings of His spirit to experience profound spiritual renewal and power.

Key Points

• Personal transformation is crucial for accessing the latter glory.

• Resistance to change often hinders spiritual progression.

• Embracing change requires submission to God's sovereignty.

• The fear of change can be overcome by understanding and embracing God's plan.

• Proper preparation for change involves repentance and realignment with God's will.

Key Themes

- **Nature of Change:** True transformation to access the latter glory involves a deep change of heart and mind, not just superficial adjustments. This change must be guided by the Holy Spirit and reflect a commitment to becoming more like Christ.
- **Fear and Resistance to Change:** Many resist change due to fear of the unknown

or comfort with the status quo, which can block the blessings and new works God wants to perform. Overcoming these fears through faith and a deeper fear of God is essential.

- **Role of God in Change:** Change should not be self-driven but must be orchestrated by God, focusing on areas that hinder our spiritual growth and effectiveness. It's about letting go of control and allowing God to lead.

- **Impact of Change on Community:** Personal change affects the wider community. When leaders and individuals embrace transformation, it can lead to a corporate entering into the latter glory, marked by signs, wonders, and deeper fellowship with God.

- **Preparation for Change:** Effective transition into the latter glory requires intentional actions such as repentance, spiritual realignment, breaking unhealthy ties, and embracing new spiritual practices that foster deeper intimacy with God.

Conclusion

The journey to the latter glory is marked by significant personal and communal transformation. This chapter serves as a guide for those seeking to not only experience God's greater glory but to become conduits of His power and presence in the world.

CHAPTER 11

WALKING UNDER THE GLORY CLOUD

Bible Verse

"And with a pillar of cloud You led them by day, and with a pillar of fire by night to light for them the way in which they were to go." (Nehemiah 9:12-13 NASB)

Introduction

This chapter explores the profound impact of living under the direct guidance and presence of God's glory cloud, drawing parallels from the experiences of the Israelites in the wilderness to modern spiritual journeys guided by God's presence.

Word of Wisdom

"No man who knows God should limit Him; this would be his greatest mistake."
Guillermo Maldonado

Main Theme

Living under the "glory cloud" symbolizes walking in God's continual presence, where His supernatural power actively operates in the lives of believers, leading to miraculous transformations and divine guidance.

Key Points

• The glory cloud represents God's tangible presence guiding and protecting His people.

• Historical and biblical events under the glory cloud demonstrate God's supernatural interventions.

• Unbelief and disobedience can hinder the blessings available under the glory cloud.

• Understanding and respecting the glory cloud is essential for experiencing its full benefits.

• The glory cloud is a symbol of God's sovereignty and power over all creation.

Key Themes

• **Divine Guidance and Protection:** Just as the Israelites were led by the glory cloud, believers today are called to follow God's presence for direction and protection. This divine guidance is crucial for navigating life's spiritual wilderness and reaching our God-given potential.

• **Historical Significance and Lessons:** The experiences of the Israelites under the glory cloud provide valuable lessons on the importance of faith and obedience. Despite witnessing numerous miracles, their repeated unbelief and rebellion resulted in severe consequences, teaching us the importance of maintaining faith in God's provisions.

- **The Sovereignty of God's Presence:** The glory cloud is not just a guide but a manifestation of God's sovereignty, illustrating His control over the natural and supernatural. This aspect challenges believers to recognize and submit to God's ultimate authority in all aspects of life.
- **Modern Implications of the Glory Cloud:** In contemporary times, the concept of the glory cloud extends beyond physical manifestations to include the spiritual presence that accompanies believers, influencing churches, communities, and personal lives with divine power and authority.
- **Preparation for Future Glory:** The chapter emphasizes the necessity for believers to prepare for the increased manifestations of God's glory in the end times, which promises even greater miracles and divine interventions than those experienced by the Israelites.

Conclusion

The chapter concludes with a call to embrace the lessons from the past and the present manifestations of the glory cloud, encouraging believers to live in a way that aligns with God's divine will and presence. This alignment ensures access to the full spectrum of God's blessings, protection, and guidance.

CHAPTER 12

CARRIERS OF THE GLORY OF GOD

Bible Verse

"For it is the God who commanded light to shine out of darkness, who has shone in our hearts to give the light of the knowledge of the glory of God in the face of Jesus Christ." (2 Corinthians 4:6)

Introduction

This final chapter inspires and challenges readers to become carriers of God's glory, transforming and impacting the world through divine presence and power, as illustrated by transformative testimonies and biblical principles.

Word of Wisdom

"Every believer is a present-day bearer of the ark of covenant." Guillermo Maldonado

Main Theme

The call to carry God's glory is a profound privilege and responsibility that transforms believers into divine instruments for showcasing God's power and grace in the world.

Key Points

• God designed humans to carry and manifest His glory.

• Historical lessons teach the importance of adhering to God's divine order for carrying His glory.

• The New Testament shifts the location of God's glory from the ark to the hearts of believers.

• Every believer has the potential to manifest God's glory through faith and obedience.

• God's glory in believers is meant to be actively shared and demonstrated in the world.

Key Themes

• **Divine Design and Potential:** Every individual is uniquely designed to be a vessel of God's glory, equipped to bring divine presence into everyday situations through faith and transformative actions.

• **Historical and Biblical Context:** Understanding the history of God's glory from the Old Testament, where it dwelt in the ark, to the New Testament, where it resides in the hearts of believers, provides a blueprint for how we should respect and carry this glory today.

- **Role of Believers as Modern-Day Levites:** Just as the Levites were chosen to carry the ark, believers are called to bear God's presence in their lives. This involves a lifestyle of holiness and dedication to manifesting God's power and love.
- **Impact of Carrying God's Glory:** Carrying God's glory transforms environments and brings about supernatural interventions, as evidenced by miracles and spiritual breakthroughs in various ministries around the world.
- **Personal Transformation and Global Impact:** By embracing their identity as carriers of God's glory, believers can cause significant changes not only in their personal lives but also in their wider communities, leading to revival and spiritual awakening.

Conclusion

Being a carrier of God's glory is not just a spiritual status but an active engagement in God's work on Earth, transforming lives and environments through His power. This chapter calls believers to rise to their divine potential, impacting the world and preparing it for the coming of Christ.